Woodlands

Cecilia Fitzsimons

Studio Editions

Contents

FRIEZE

Front:
A Woodland Walk
Back:
Tree Check List
Things to do ● Useful Addresses

First published in 1992 by Studio Editions Ltd,
Princess House, 50 Eastcastle Street,
London W1N 7AP, England

Text and Illustrations copyright © 1992
Cecilia Fitzsimons
Illustration credits: Cecilia Fitzsimons, pp. 4-9,
18-34, back of tree frieze. Tricia Newell, pp. 1, 3,
10-17, front of tree frieze.

All rights reserved.
ISBN 1 85170 8707
Printed and bound in Hong Kong

What is a Tree?

A tree is a tall, lasting plant with a thick, wooden trunk. Many trees growing together form woodlands and forests. In temperate lands, where it is not too hot or too cold, woodlands cover vast areas.

BROAD-LEAVED TREES

Broad-leaved trees have wide leaves that usually fall off in Winter and grow again in Spring. Some have flowers with **petals (1)**. Others have **male catkins (2)** and small **female flowers (3)**.

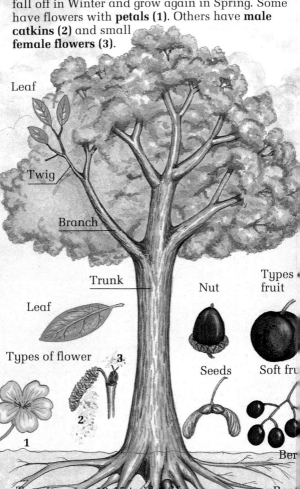

Leaf

Twig

Branch

Trunk

Leaf

Types of flower

3.

2

1

Nut

Seeds

Types fruit

Soft fru

Ber

Root

Turn to pages 10-15 to identify some common broad-leaved trees.

CONIFER TREES

Conifer trees have long, narrow leaves like needles. Most conifers do not lose their leaves in Winter, so we call them **evergreen trees**. Instead of flowers, conifers have small **female cones (4)** and yellow **male cones (5)** that release clouds of pollen. Female cones grow large and eventually release tiny seeds.

Branch

Twig

Trunk

Fully grown cone

Leaves

5

"Flowers" are cones

Seed

Turn to pages 16-17 to identify some common conifers.

Roots

5

The Woodland Year

Broad-leaved trees undergo great changes at different times of the year. Conifers hardly change at all.

Spring

Summer

Broad-leaved trees sprout new leaves and flowers. Plants flower beneath the trees before the light is blocked by the leaves growing above.

Broad-leaved trees are i full leaf, some in flower Beneath, it is shaded and the ground is covered with Bracken and other plants.

Autumn

Winter

he trees are heavy with uit or nuts. As the days et shorter and colder e leaves change colour nd die.

Broad-leaved trees stand bare without their leaves. Conifers and a few evergreen broad-leaved trees stay green.

Life in the Woods

Woodlands and forests provide homes, protection and food for many animals and birds. Woodland plants, from tiny flowers to tall trees, create different layers where animals can live. The layers are like the floors of a house.

ATTIC

The tree-top is like the **attic**. Birds and insects live here. Some butterflies only fly around the tops of trees. Birds nest on the **top floor**, in the middle of the tree. Small mammals like squirrels search for food and make their homes here too.

TOP FLOOR

Upstairs includes the lower level of the tree; its trunk and the small trees and bushes nearby. Woodpeckers and other birds search here for insects.

UPSTAIRS

Downstairs, on the ground, are homes for many animals, from insects to deer, which live and feed amongst the plants that grow here.

DOWNSTAIRS

CELLAR

Underground, in the **cellar**, animals like foxes, badgers and rabbits make burrows. Insects and worms live in the soil.

8

Many birds live in woodlands. Turn to page 20 to find out more.

Many mammals live in woodlands. Find them on page 22.

Temperate woodlands are found all over the world. To find out about the different plants and animals turn to pages 24-31.

Many beautiful insects live in or near trees. Young caterpillars eat the leaves, and larvae burrow into wood and bark. They are eaten by many birds. To find out more, turn to page 18.

When plants and animals die they rot and the nutrients pass into roots to help trees and plants grow. Fungi and insects break down wood and leaf litter.

Leaf litter

Simple Leaves

Trees can be identified by the shape and size of their leaves. The simplest have a basic oval shape with smooth or toothed edges.

Hornbeam (1) leaves are toothed. Tiny nutlets have leafy scales. **Beech (2)** catkins are yellow pom-poms. Triangular nuts grow in spiky cases.

Silver Birch (3) has white bark. Twigs hang down; catkins in Spring.

One of many similar poplars, the **Lombardy Poplar (4)** is tall and thin. Catkins appear before the leaves.

The **Holm Oak (5)** is an unusual evergreen oak tree with simple oval leaves.

Lime (6) has heart-shaped leaves. Flower clusters hang beneath a leafy scale.

Sweet Chestnut (7) trees grow edible chestnuts in spiky cases. The leaves are long and toothed and the catkins flower in early Summer.

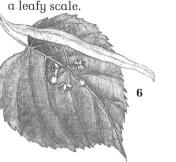

8

9

These trees flower before their leaves appear. **Pussy Willow (8)**, a common bush or small tree, has furry grey catkins. The **Judas Tree (9)** has pea-like flowers and pods.

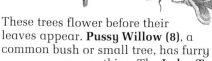

10

Tasmanian Blue Gum (10) has young round leaves and older long ones.

11

Rhododendron (11) trees, from the Himalayas and U.S.A., have colourful flower clusters.

2

Beautiful **Magnolia (12)** trees from China and U.S.A. have huge flowers and leaves.

13

Tupelo (13) is an ornamental tree from America. In Autumn the leaves turn bright red.

The **Indian Bean Tree (14)** with its wide leaves is planted to give shade. It has long brown seed pods.

15

14

Hazel (15) trees give us hazelnuts. Long catkins appear before the leaves in Spring.

Leaves with Many Sides

Some leaves grow into irregular shapes. Their edges may be toothed, spiky, rounded lobes or shaped like a hand.

Like other oak trees, the **English Oak (1)** has lobed leaves, acorns and tassel-like catkins. Trees live for over 500 years.

Red Oak (2) comes from North America where there are many species. Its spiky leaves turn dark red in Autumn.

Holly (3) is well known at Christmas time for its spiny leaves and bright red berries.

The **Tulip Tree (4)** has square leaves and flowers like tulips. It comes from North America.

London Planes (5), are planted as street trees. They have flaky, mottled bark, hand-shaped leaves and round fruits.

Fossil Trees (6) are one of the oldest types of tree and first appeared before the age of the dinosaurs. Their leaves are found as fossils.

6

7

There are many types of palm tree which mostly grow in warm climates. The **Windmill Palm (7)** can bear colder weather, so it is often planted in Northern Europe.

8

Fig (8) trees are grown for their wrinkly, purple fruit. Common in Southern Europe, they will produce fruit in the North in a warm place.

9

Sassafras (9) leaves are plain oval or shaped like three fingers. It comes from North America and is planted as a shade tree in Europe.

10

11

Many **Japanese Maples (10)** have coloured leaves. Their winged fruits, called keys, spin like helicopters as they fall. In Europe, tall **Sycamores (11)** grow quickly.

13

Divided Leaves

These trees have large leaves which are each divided up into many smaller leaflets.

The **Tree of Heaven (1)** comes from China, but is common in Europe where it is planted in parks, gardens and along roads. Each leaflet has a pair of 'teeth' at its base. Clusters of greenish flowers produce many winged fruits.

The common **Mountain Ash (2)** grows wild on mountains. The red berries are eaten by birds in Winter.

Elder (3) is found in woodlands and hedgerows. Clusters of flowers and black berries are both used to make wine.

The **Locust Tree (4)** from North America has white pea-like flowers and brown pods. In Europe it is often planted in parks and gardens and along roadsides.

Mimosa (5) leaves are greatly divided and fern-like. Perfumed flowers, like yellow pom-poms, hang in long clusters. Originally from Australia, these trees are common in Southern Europe. In England they survive in a few frost-free areas on the South Coast.

The **Shagbark Hickory (6)**, named for its flaky bark, is an American tree grown for its wood and planted in gardens in Europe. It is related to Walnuts and Pecans.

Sumachs (7) come from Europe and U.S.A. They are planted in parks and gardens in Britain and often escape to grow wild nearby. The leaves are very long and may have up to 21 leaflets. The flowers are dark red, furry spikes.

Walnut (8) leaves have up to nine leaflets. The edible walnuts grow inside a leathery green case. The wood has beautiful patterns and is used for the finest furniture.

Leaves Like Needles

Conifer trees have leaves like needles. These may be long and thin or short and flat. Some leaves are very small and scale-like. Leaves are arranged on the stem in different patterns, in rows, whorls or clusters.

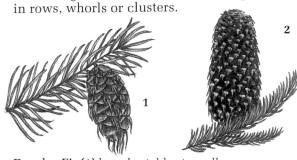

Douglas Fir (1) has short, blunt needles with cones on the branch tips. These tall North American trees are grown for timber in Europe. The **Noble Fir (2)**, also from North America, has bluish needles and large cones.

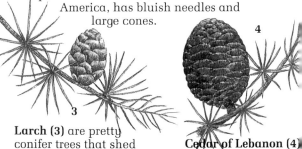

Larch (3) are pretty conifer trees that shed their leaves in Winter. The small cones sit upright.

Cedar of Lebanon (4) has wide curved branches. Large flat-topped cones ooze sticky resin

The **Sitka Spruce (5)** from North America is grown in Europe. **Norway Spruce (6)** is the familiar Christmas tree. It bears long cigar-shaped cones.

Western Red Cedar (7) from North America gives us cedar wood. Ferny branchlets are covered with short scale leaves. Its cones are tiny.

7

8

Scots Pine (8) is the native pine tree of Europe and Northern Asia. It has a straight trunk and a wide top. The pointed needles grow in pairs. Cones hang downwards.

Juniper (9) cones are unusual. They look like berries and are used to flavour gin. The tree is small and shrubby. Its short, flat needles are sharp and are widely spaced in whorls of 3.

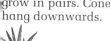

9

10

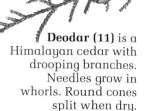

Leyland Cypress (10) is a garden tree bred by nurserymen. It is now grown everywhere. It has short ferny branchlets covered with small scale leaves. The small round cones have no more than 8 scales.

Deodar (11) is a Himalayan cedar with drooping branches. Needles grow in whorls. Round cones split when dry.

11

12

Western Hemlock (12) from North America is grown in parks and for its wood. The leaves are flat. Small cones grow down from the branch tips.

Insects

Trees provide food and homes for thousands of woodland insects which lay their eggs on leaves or in bark. These hatch into caterpillar or larvae which feed on the tree. The young eventually change into adult insects.

Cicadas (1) *35mm* are large bugs that suck plant juices. They chirp loudly in the sun. Common in Southern Europe, one species lives in the New Forest in England.

The **Hornet (2)** *35mm* looks like a large orange wasp. It is not aggressive unless disturbed.

The **Ichneumon Fly (3)** *35mm* is a wasp whose young feed on the living larvae of other insects that burrow through wood.

Stag Beetles (4) *80mm* live near old Oak trees where the larvae gnaw into stumps and old wood. The males have huge jaws used for fighting.

Wood Ants (5) *18mm* collect bits of leaf and twigs to build a huge mounded nest.
These creatures are not insects: the **Woodlouse (6)** *18mm* and **Millipede (7)** *40mm* live in leaf litter. **Wolf Spiders (8)** *8mm* search the forest floor for prey.

18

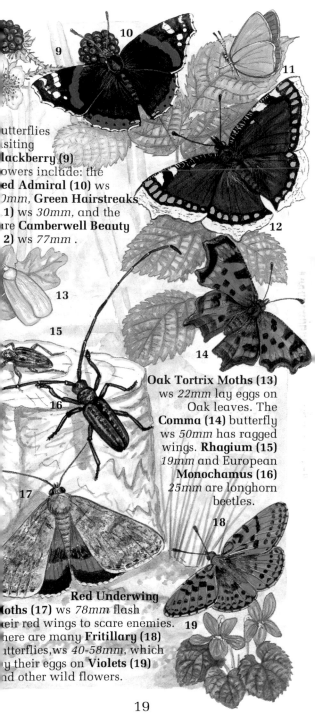

utterflies
siting
lackberry (9)
owers include: the
ed Admiral (10) ws
0mm, **Green Hairstreaks
1)** ws *30mm*, and the
re **Camberwell Beauty
2)** ws *77mm* .

Oak Tortrix Moths (13)
ws *22mm* lay eggs on
Oak leaves. The
Comma (14) butterfly
ws *50mm* has ragged
wings. **Rhagium (15)**
19mm and European
Monochamus (16)
25mm are longhorn
beetles.

**Red Underwing
oths (17)** ws *78mm* flash
eir red wings to scare enemies.
here are many **Fritillary (18)**
tterflies, ws *40-58mm*, which
y their eggs on **Violets (19)**
nd other wild flowers.

Birds

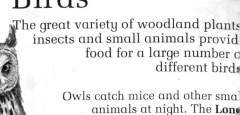

The great variety of woodland plants
insects and small animals provid
food for a large number o
different bird

Owls catch mice and other sma
animals at night. The **Lon**
Eared Owl (1) *36cm* spend
the day resting close to th
trunk of a tree

Tawny Owls (2
38cm nest i
hollow tree
They also ea
birds an
insect

The secretive **Goshawk (3)**
60cm lives in woodlands and
conifer forests. It nests in trees
and catches quite large birds
and mammals to eat.

In Northern pine
forests and Birch
woods, **Waxwings**
(4) *18 cm* search
through trees for
insects and berries.
In Winter large flocks
of these pretty birds
travel southwards and
can be seen in gardens.

The **Song Thrush (**
23cm lives in woo
and gardens, nestin
in a tree or hedge.
sings beautifull
sitting high
the tree top

Buzzards (6) *56cm* live in the West and North of Britain. When you hear their cat-like mewing cry, look for them soaring high above the tree tops. They catch rabbits to eat.

There are many small birds in the forest. The **Crossbill (7)** *16cm* uses its crossed bill to get the seeds out of fir cones. The tiny **Firecrest (8)** *9cm* and its relative the **Goldcrest** are Europe's smallest birds. The **Wren (9)** *9.5cm* is a little larger. The **Marsh Tit (10)** *11cm* searches amongst twigs and leaves for food.

Lesser Spotted Woodpeckers (11) *14cm* drill into wood for insects, and to make nest holes. Males have a red patch of feathers on top of the head. **Pheasants (12)** *89cm* cannot fly well. They nest on the ground in **Bracken (13)** *2m* and other plants.

The **Nuthatch (14)** *14cm* runs head first down a tree trunk looking for insects hidden in the bark. It also eats nuts and seeds. **Treecreepers (15)** *12.5cm* creep up the tree and nest in small spaces behind the bark.

Mammals

Woodlands and forests provide cover and shelter for large animals. Deer and other animals can hide in the woods and often live quite close to people's houses.

Large Red Deer (1) *2.6m* live in forests and parks. **Grey Squirrels (2)** *54cm* from America are now common in Southern England.

Fireweed (3) *1.2m* grows in clearings after a fire. **Oak Bracket Fungus (4)** *40cm* grows on old Oak wood.

Rabbits (5) *45cm* dig complicated burrows in soft soil under trees and bushes. They graze on grass in clearings and fields.

The **Wood Mouse (6)** *20cm* hides by day, and feeds at night. **Liverwort (7)** and **Moss (8)** are flat, simple plants that grow in damp places.

Chantarelle (9) **Cep (10)** and **Morel (11)** are edible fungi. Always ask an expert to show you which species are not poisonous. Tiny **Shrews (12)** *8cm* eat insects and other small creatures.

In Europe **Bears (13)** *2.5m* are rare now, and are found mainly in the North.

Pine Martens (14) *80cm* are predators that live in pine forests. The rare **Lynx (15)** *1.3m* is a large cat with a short tail, from Europe, America and, Asia.

The **Wolf (16)** *2m* lives in packs in Eastern Europe and parts of the South. They hunt deer but may attack farm animals.

The **Red Fox (17)** *1.2m* is common and now also lives in towns. At night it hunts for any food.

Wild Boar (18) *1.8m* are common on the Continent. At night they visit nearby fields. They love to suck the juice from grapes.

Weasels (19) *25cm* are small, fierce predators. They eat small animals like mice and baby birds.

Many different **Ferns (20)** *45cm* grow in damp woodlands. **Voles (21)** *17cm* are like short, fat mice. They live in shallow burrows dug in grassy woodland clearings.

Europe

Conifer forests grow in the colder North and on mountains. Where it is warmer, most woods contain broad-leaved trees. Pine and Holm Oak trees grow in the hot Mediterranean.

Ash (1) has divided leaves and leafy keys. The wood is used for furniture. **English Elm (2)** suffer from Dutch Elm Disease. The fruit has small round wings.

Yew (3) is the dark conifer seen in churchyards and woodlands. Its seeds sit in a fleshy pink cup. The **Green Woodpecker (4)** *32cm* has a loud laughing cry.

The pretty **Fat Dormouse (5)** *35cm* used to be kept and eaten by the Romans. It lives like a squirrel in trees. A few live in England.

The **Wildcat (6)** *65cm* looks like a tabby cat. It lives in the mountain forests of Scotland and in other parts of Europe and Africa. **Red Squirrels (7)** *45cm* mostly live in the North and West of Britain. Elsewhere in Europe, some are almost black in colour.

24

Serbian Spruce (8)
can live in polluted air.
Horse Chestnuts (9) have
"candles" of flowers and poisonous
nuts, called "Conkers". The **Silver
Fir (10)** has large upright cones.

Hawthorn (11) has
pink or white flowers
and dark red berries.
Fallow Deer (12) *1.5m*
have wide, flat antlers.
Roe Deer (13) *1.2m*
have small antlers.

The **Badger (14)** *1m*
digs a large set. Look
for earth piled up
outside.

The **Purple Emperor (15)** ws *65mm*
and the **Speckled Wood (16)** ws *44mm*
butterflies bask in sunny clearings. The
Bluebell (17) *50cm*, **Foxglove (18)**
1.5m, and **Primrose (19)** *15cm*
are pretty woodland flowers.

North America

Many North American trees are now grown all over the world. Some kinds of American woodland animal have become known worldwide because they have been used as characters in cartoons.

The **Paper Birch (1)** has pretty white bark that peels off. It is planted in Europe as a garden tree. The leaf **(a)** looks like Silver Birch. **White-tailed Deer (2)** *1.8m* flash their tails when frightened.

White Pine (3) is an important tree for wood and paper mills. It is called the Weymouth Pine in Europe. **Long-leaf Pine (4)** has very long needles. It gives us turpentine and resin.

Racoons (5) *90cm* eat small animals and fruits. Some live in Germany

Pileated Woodpecker (6) *43cm* has a ringing call.

Tassel-eared Squirrels (7) *58cm* have long tufts on their ears. They live in conifer forests in the West

The **Sugar Maple (8)** gives us Maple
Syrup and fine wood for furniture.
White Oak (9) and **Post Oak (10)** are
common Oaks used for timber.

The **Paw Paw (11)** fruit tastes
like custard.

The **Opossum (12)** *75cm* is a marsupial;
its babies grow in a pouch. The **Skunk (13)**
1.2m scares away enemies by spraying a
smelly liquid at them. The **Flicker (14)** *30cm*
is a type of woodpecker. **Whip-Poor-Will (15)**
25cm rests on the ground. At night
it flies to catch insects.

Flowering Dogwood (16) trees
flower in Spring. The pretty
Chipmunk (17) *30cm* is a
small squirrel with stripes
down its side.

Tiger Swallowtail (18)
ws *14cm* is a common
woodland butterfly.

Asia

Many exotic animals and plants live in the forests of the Far East, in China and Japan. In Victorian times explorers travelled to these areas to collect plants for their gardens in Britain, Europe and America.

The **Flying Squirrel (1)** *30cm* lives in Northern conifer forests of both Europe and Asia. It glides with furry flaps of skin stretched between its legs.

Small **Muntjak Deer (2)** *90cm* have short antlers. They have been introduced into Britain and France.

Handkerchief Tree (3) flowers have leafy petals like hankies. **Loquat (4)** have large leaves and orange fruit. Both are grown in Europe.

Golden Pheasant (5) *1.1m* have golden feathers. They live in the mountainous woodlands of China and have been introduced into Southern England.

The **Red Panda (6)** *1.2m* lives in Bamboo forests and rests during the day, high in the tops of a tree. The **Sable (7)** *1m* is related to the Pine Marten.

Bamboo (8) is a tall, grass-like plant which we use for garden canes and furniture.

Tigers (9) *3.7m* are endangered animals. They may become extinct if we do not protect them. **Sika Deer (10)** *1.2m* from China and Japan, live in parks in Europe.

Japanese White Pine (11) is the spidery tree seen in Japanese gardens and on Willow Pattern plates.

Japanese Flowering Cherries (12) are known in gardens all over the world. There are many varieties. This one, called Kanzan is one of the most popular in Britain.

Australia

Temperate woodlands are found in Eastern Australia. The trees and animals that live there are very different from those seen in Europe, Asia and America. Many trees are Eucalyptus, normally called Gum trees. Most of the mammals are marsupials.

Kookaburras (1) *47cm* are large kingfishers. They catch snakes and other small animals.

The tiny **Blossom Bat (2)** *5cm* feeds on the nectar from flowers, fruit and insects.

Parrots and their relatives are common in Australia. The **Sulphur-crested Cockatoo (3)** *50cm* can be seen in large flocks. **Native Box (4)** is a small tree with white flowers.

The **Tiger Cat (5)** *77cm* is one of several marsupial cats. All are rare and are being pushed out by people and the animals they have taken to Australia. The **Fat-tailed Dunnart (6)** *8cm* is a marsupial mouse. The **Hairpin Banksia (7)** shrub has bottle-brush flowers

Most Gum trees look alike. Only the fruits circled are different. **Red Gum (8)** has long thin leaves, **Snow Gum (9)** has short fat ones. **Sydney Blue Gum (10)** is common in the East and is the favourite food of the **Koala Bear (11)** *80cm*. Mother Koalas carry babies on their backs.

Grey Kangaroos (12) *1.5m* rest during the day and graze on grass at night. A baby Kangaroo is called a "Joey". The **Native Apricot (13)** is a small tree with yellow flowers and sticky orange fruits.

The *75cm* long tail feathers of the male **Lyrebird (14)** 25cm, are used to attract a female. The tail is opened in display in a little clearing about ⅓m wide.

Man and the Forest

From the earliest times people have used trees to build shelters to protect them from the weather. Nowadays we cut wood for building, paper-making and many other uses. Trees also provide us with food, oils and other products like medicines.

The natural forests must be protected and managed because people use tonnes of wood every year. Fast-growing trees from countries like America are grown in plantations around the worl

Animals and Plants in Danger

These plants and animals are rare and may become extinct if we do not protect them.

Lady's Slipper Orchid (1).
Although still fairly common in North America, these beautiful flowers are rare and protected in Europe. They only grow in one place in Britain and are closely guarded.

Pollution

Pollution is caused by anything that people do that changes the natural world around them.

Air pollution is especially bad for trees and plants. We pollute the air with smoke from our homes, factories and cars.

When we burn coal and oil, gases are set free and escape into the sky. Here they turn water into tiny droplets of acid which falls as acid rain, killing trees. Large areas of forest in Europe and North America are being damaged.

Chemicals called CFCs escape from aerosol cans and fridges. They damage the ozone layer which protects us from the harmful rays of the sun. These rays damage baby seedlings and affect plant growth.

What can you do to help?.....
See page 34

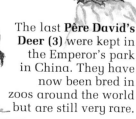

The **Spanish Imperial Eagle (2)** is endangered. It builds a large nest at the top of a tall tree.

The last **Père David's Deer (3)** were kept in the Emperor's park in China. They have now been bred in zoos around the world but are still very rare.

Glossary

Catkin A flower without petals, usually male, sometimes female.

Fungi Non-flowering plant that usually feeds on other animals or plants.

Insect Has a body in 3 parts, 3 pairs jointed legs, 2 pairs wings.

Introduced Plant or animal brought to one country from another.

Mammal Warm furry animals; their babies drink mothers' milk.

Marsupial Mammal with a furry pouch in which babies grow.

Nutrients Substances used as food.

Ornamental Beautiful garden tree or shrub.

Species A type of animal or plant.

Whorl A ring of leaves.

ws = wingspan

Measurements given for animals and plants are the longest or tallest usually seen; many examples are smaller. Animals are measured from nose to tail.

Conservation

What can **you** do to help take care of your environment?

1. Recycle and reuse paper and cardboard, and you will save trees. Many charities sell labels to stick on to envelopes, so that you can send them through the post again.

2. Encourage your family and friends to buy wooden products made only from wood from "sustainable forests" (where for every tree cut down another one is planted).

3. Try to select ozone-friendly products. Choose pump-action sprays rather than aerosols.

4. Support woodland conservation projects and wildlife groups and zoos breeding endangered species.

5. Observe the Countryside Code. Do not pick wild flowers or dig up trees. Try not to disturb wild birds and animals.

BE A WOODLAND DETECTIVE

As you walk through the woods, look for clues to the mammals that live there.
(1) Black-and-white hair from a Badger.
(2) Bark stripped by Rabbits and Deer.
(3) Tracks left in soft mud or snow.
(4) Plum-sized Deer droppings.
(5) Pea-sized Rabbit droppings.
Hazelnuts, chewed by Voles **(6)**, Mice **(7)**, and Squirrels **(8)**.
Squirrels also eat fir cones **(9)**.

CAN YOU FIND THESE PRINTS?

Dog

Fox

Squirrel

Deer

GROW A TREE

Collect nuts and seeds in Autumn.
1. Fill a flower pot with compost. Place the nut in the middle. Press down the compost, and water well.
2. Water regularly and a seedling tree with two leaves will soon grow. When your baby tree gets too big for its pot you can plant it outside.

1

2

BARK RUBBING

Take a piece of paper and hold it firmly against a tree trunk with one hand. Using the other hand, rub over the paper with a wax crayon or soft pencil. The pattern of the bark will appear on the paper.

Use the same method to make leaf rubbings. You may have to put the leaf on a hard flat surface.

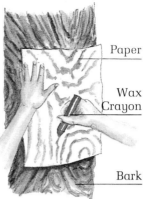

Paper

Wax Crayon

Bark

CAN YOU FIND THESE TREES?

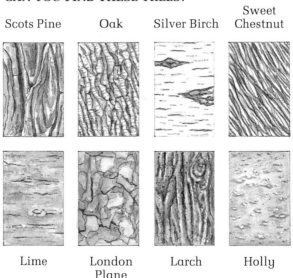

Scots Pine   Oak   Silver Birch   Sweet Chestnut

Lime   London Plane   Larch   Holly

TREE RINGS

At the end of a log, the wood has a pattern of tree rings in it. One or more are grown by every tree each year. Count the rings and tell how old a tree is.

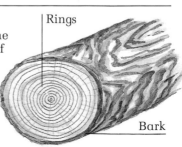

Rings

Bark

Things to do

Woodlands and forests are great places to walk and play in. They are full of mystery; we can never be sure what we will see around the next corner ... maybe, a Fox or a Deer. Here are some things to look for and to do when you next visit the woods.

NATURE NOTES
Keep a nature notebook or diary. It will help you to remember all that you have seen. Make drawings and write about leaves, insects, birds - in fact anything that interests you.

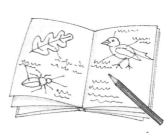

SPRING
Look for flowers and catkins on the trees. How many types can you see....flowers, catkins, tassles, pom-poms, others?

SUMMER
Sit quietly in a sunny clearing and watch butterflies. Where do they land - on flowers, fruit, trees, the ground or by puddles?

AUTUMN
Collect fallen leaves. Press them flat between tissue paper and under a pile of books. Then stick them onto paper or card.

WINTER
Different trees have different shaped twigs and buds. **London Plane (1)**, **Beech (2)**, **Oak (3)**, **Pussy Willow (4)**.

EVERGREEN TREES

Norway Spruce
Conical, *65m*.
Needles, *2.5cm*.
Long scaly cones,
18cm. Greyish
bark splits into
flaky plates. (p 16)

Sitka Spruce
Conical, *60m*
high. Needles
3cm. Soft, scaly
cones, *10cm*. Bark
greyish with flaky
plates. (p 16)

Serbian Spruce
Narrow, *30m* high.
Needles *2cm*.
Blackish cones,
6cm. Reddish bark
flaky and papery.
(p 25)

Western Hemlock
Conical tree, *70m*
high. Needles
2cm long. Scaly
cones, *2.5cm*.
Reddish, split
bark. (p 17)

Douglas Fir
Tall conical tree,
100m. Needles
3.5cm. Cones
10cm, scaly,
spiky.Grey
bark. (p 16)

Scots Pine
Rounded top,
50m. Needles in
pairs, *8cm*. Grey
woody cones,
8cm. Reddish
bark. (p 17)

**White or
Weymouth Pine**
Conical, *50m*.
Long needles
14cm, in groups
of 2-5. Long cone,
20cm. (p 26)

Holly
Small, rounded,
10m. Spiky
leaves, *12cm*.
White flowers,
8mm. Red berries,
1cm. (p 12)

Holm Oak
Rounded *25m*.
Dark green oval
leaves, *10cm*.
Acorns in deep
cups. Brown
bark. (p 10)

Magnolia
Evergreen species
30m. Oval leaves,
16cm. Large
creamy flowers,
25cm. July -
November. (p 11)

Rhododendron
Shrub or tree.
Some *12m*.
Smooth oval
leaves, *15cm*.
Flowers, *6cm*
wide. (p 11)

Loquat
Shrub or tree,
10m. Long leaves,
25cm. Furry
twigs, white
flowers, orange
fruits, 6cm. (p 28)

Mimosa
Tree or shrub,
30m. Ferny
leaves. Yellow
pom-pom flowers.
Flat pods, *10cm*.
Green bark. (p 15)

**Tasmanian
Blue Gum**
Rounded, *65m*.
Curved leaves,
30cm. White
flowers, white
peeling bark. (p 11)

Red Gum
Loose rounded,
40mm. Leaves,
slightly curved,
22cm. Cream
flowers. Creamy
peeling bark. (p 31)

Windmill Palm
14m. Straight
trunk, leaves at
top, fan-like 1m
across. Black
fruits, *2cm*.
(p 13)

Japanese Maple
Small, round shrub or tree, *14m*. Leaves *9cm*, up to 11 "fingers". Varieties: purple,

green, white. Red or yellow in Autumn. (p 13)

Handkerchief Tree
Small, round, *20m*. Heart-shaped leaves, *18cm*.

Flowers like large white "hankies", *15cm*. Round fruits, *3.5cm*. (p 28)

Sassafras
Rounded, *18m*. Leaves oval or 3-pointed, *13cm*. Yellowish flowers,

black berries, *1cm*. Grey ridged bark. Planted as a shade tree. (p 13)

Tupelo
Tall, rounded, *30m*. Oval leaves, *15cm*. Bright red and yellow in Autumn.

Flowers green. Black fruits, *1cm*. Grey, ridged bark. (p 11)

Yew
Wide conical tree, *25m* high. Flat needles, *4cm* long. Seed in red cup, *1cm*. Red bark. (p 24)

Leyland Cypress
Tall, narrow tree, *35m* high. Scale leaves, *2mm* long. Cones are rare. Dark red-brown bark. (p 17)

Juniper
Wide, conical shrub or tree, *15m* high. Pointed needles, *2cm* long. Blue-black berries, *9 cm*. (p 17)

Western Red Cedar
Narrow pyramid, *65m*. Leaves are *3mm*-long scales. Tiny cones *12mm*. (p 17)

Silver Fir
A tall pyramid, *50m* high. Needles *3cm* long. Cones *20cm*. Bark, grey brown and scaly. (p 25)

Noble Fir
Conical, *80m*. Bluish-green needles, *3.5cm* long. Fat cones, *20cm*. Bark, greyish, smooth. (p 16)

Deodar
Conical tree, *65m* high. Branches droop. Needles *5cm* long. Rounded cones, *12cm*. Bark grey-brown. (p 17)

Cedar of Lebanon
Wide, rounded, flat top, *40m* high. Needles *3cm* long. Cones, *12cm*. Greyish split bark. (p 16)

DECICUOUS TREES

Elder
Round tree or shrub, *10m*. Divided leaves, 5-7 leaflets each *12cm*.

White flower umbrella, *24cm*. Black berries, *6mm*. Grey grooved bark. (p 14)

Locust Tree
Loose, rounded, *25m*. Divided leaves, up to 21 leaflets each *4.5cm*.

Sprays of white pea flowers. Pods, *10cm*. Grey ridged bark. (p 14)

Tree of Heaven
Loose, round, *20m*. Divided leaves, up to 25 leaflets each *12cm*.

Green flowers. Leafy fruit, *4cm*. Grey bark, smooth or scaly. (p 14)

Sumach
Small, round, *10m*. Divided leaves, up to 21 leaflets each *12cm*. Dark

red,furry flower head, *10cm*. Brown fruit, some stay on tree in winter. (p.15)

Fig
Low, spreading tree or shrub, *10m*. Hand-like leaves, *20cm*. Fruit, pear-shaped, *8cm*.

Smooth grey bark. Thick green twigs, large pointed buds, round leaf scars. (p 13)

Tulip Tree
Tall, slim, rounded, *45m*. Square leaf, *20cm*. Red in Autumn. Cream and orange

flowers, *6cm*. Mass of winged seeds, *8.5cm*. Bark grey. (p 12)

Japanese Cherry
Small, round, *15m*. Oval leaves, *20cm*. Masses of flowers. Varieties: "Kanzan" pink,

rose-like, *1.5cm*; "Amanagowa", tall thin tree, pale pink flowers; others - white or pink. (p 29)

Judas Tree
Small, round, *10m*. Round leaves, *12cm*. Pink pea flowers in May before

leaves appear. Flowers sometimes sprout on trunk and branches. Pod, *10cm*. (p 11)

DECIDUOUS TREES

Hazel
Round tree or
shrub, *12m.*
Heart-shaped
leaves, *12cm.*
Catkins 8cm.

Hazelnuts, *2cm,*
grow in leafy
cups. Smooth
brown bark.
(p 11)

Beech
Large, broad tree,
40m. Oval leaves,
10cm. Pom-pom
catkins. Nuts
1.8cm in spiky

case. Smooth grey
bark. Thin zig-zag
twigs, pointed
buds. (p 10)

Hornbeam
Rounded tree,
30m. Oval leaves,
10cm. Catkins
5cm. Cluster of
leafy nutlets.

Grey split bark.
Thin zig-zag
twigs, small
scaly buds.
(p 10)

Sweet Chestnut
Rounded tree-
top, *30m.* Long
toothed leaves,
25cm. Yellow
catkins, *25cm.*

Nuts in spiky case.
Grey brown bark,
twisted and split.
Twigs have small
buds with large
leaf scars. (p 10)

Horse Chestnut
Rounded tree, *25m.*
Leaves divided into
5-7 leaflets, *25cm.*
White flower spike.
Fruit is poisonous

"conker". Grey
bark. Large twigs
with red sticky
buds. Large leaf
scars. (p 25)

English Oak
Rounded tree,
45m. Heavy
twisted branches.
Lobed leaves,
12cm. Tassel

catkins. "Acorn"
nut in cup. Grey
bark splits. Twigs
with several buds
at tip. (p 12)

Red Oak
Rounded tree,
35m. Pointed leaf,
22cm. Dark red in
Autumn. Yellow
catkins. Acorn in

shallow cup.
Smooth grey
bark. Twigs with
several buds at
tip. (p 12)

English Elm
Narrow, rounded,
35m. Oval leaves,
10cm. No flower
petals. Round flat
fruit, *1.7cm.*

Brown bark, splits
into squares. Thin
zig-zag twigs; tiny
buds. (p 24)

DECIDUOUS TREES

Shagbark Hickory
Rounded tree, *40m*. 5 leaflets, each *20cm*. Catkins, *15cm*.

Walnut-like fruits, *6cm*. Grey bark strips into long scales. (p 15)

London Plane
Rounded, *35m*. Leaves, hand-like, *24cm*. Round fruit breaks up into seeds. Bark flaky,

peels in coloured patches. Zig-zag twigs with brown buds. (p 12)

Sycamore
Wide, rounded, *35m*. Hand-like leaves, *15cm*. Clusters of yellow flowers, *12cm*.

Pairs of winged keys, *6cm* wide. Grey, split bark. Twigs have pairs of green buds. (p 13)

Lime
Rounded tree, *46m*. Heart-shaped leaves, *10cm*. Clusters of yellow flowers.

Round fruits, *8mm*. Grey bark, fine splits. Thin twigs, buds with 2 scales. (p 10)

Hawthorn
Small round tree, *18m*. Leaves, 3-5 points, *4.5cm*. White or pink flowers, *1.5cm*

in clusters. Berries red *1.4cm*. Split grey bark. Spiny twigs. (p 25)

Mountain Ash
Irregular tree, *20m*. Leaves divided, up to 17 leaflets, each *6cm*. Large umbrella of

white flowers. Red fruit, *9mm*. Smooth grey bark. (p 14)

Ash
Rounded, *40m*. Divided leaves *35cm*, up to 13 leaflets. Purplish flowers. Leafy

fruit, *5cm*. Bark, grey, smooth or split. Thick grey twigs with black buds. (p 24)

Indian Bean Tree
Wide, rounded, *20m*. Large, heart-shaped leaves, *25cm*. White flower sprays,

5cm wide. Brown beans, *40cm*. Smooth grey bark. (p 11)